I0478876

Info business-Fast Startup.

Guide for beginners info businessmen.

Create your own online business!

*Expert Email-Marketing
Oleg Kolpakov.*

Content:

Expert Email-Marketing
Oleg Kolpakov.

Entry:

Info business is the sale of useful information and knowledge!

Are you interested in the topic of learning on the Internet?

Then be sure to read this book!

Are you just starting your business info?

Then this book will be useful for you!

Here a lot of interesting and useful information for beginner's info businessmen.

This book describes the process of creating and maintaining info business online.

Read this book and you will no longer need to spend time and find more information.

Expert Email-Marketing
Oleg Kolpakov.

If the book you'll learn how to organize your online business and achieve the desired result.

A book you will help you to save time and money.

In the book a large amount of practical information to start business info.

Here is a detailed step-by-step plan of action.

Knowledge from this book will enable you to acquire basic concepts in the field of Internet business.

Tips and tricks will make your online experience convenient, easy.

Avoid the many pitfalls and get the desired effect in business info.

Introduction:

Hello, dear reader.

Thank you for choosing one of my books.

I promise to share with you valuable and useful information that will change your life if you all do in practice.

In the book practical actions that you need to commit to arranging this business!

I tried to make a book in a small volume, not too boring, and no necessary details and brief the upcoming events.

Studying the manual, you will have time to understand a subject that you have to deal with in the future.

This guide will be your first instrument, having studied it, you can easily understand and all the other, more complex and more powerful tools.

Expert Email-Marketing
Oleg Kolpakov.

Before I didn't know what Info business and earn money online, but thought, how you can change your life for the better.

Then I learned about info business, thanks to the Internet.

In the beginning, I found it difficult to find all the information and understand it yourself, it takes a long time.

Now to me this is the main lesson of my life.

In another area of life, I no longer see myself.

Info business for me has become the main source of income.

Hope that info business you enjoy, like me.

Today Info business is the new reality of a future of peace for me.

Now, in the modern world, all work on the automation of Business Info for

*Expert Email-Marketing
Oleg Kolpakov.*

you perform robots and computer programs.

I know that in the future, all businesses of the world will be driven out of the House, behind the laptop or computer.

Now I want to help you go through and make this difficult path info businessman thanks, this practical guidance in this book.

All the tips and tricks from my personal experience and I will help you organize your own online business, without errors and as quickly as possible!

Ready to start? Then let's get started!

Advantage Business Info:

You can work anywhere, traveling and on vacation. You only need a laptop and the Internet.

Great coverage, will enable you to earn good money anywhere in the world.

Don't need work and monitoring staff.

Selection of themes for the boundary is not implemented in info business that will allow you to increase your income.

It is not difficult because the process is automated business info.

Info business does not require any special knowledge and there are no age restrictions.

You'll work only for yourself, there will be no Chief.

Expert Email-Marketing
Oleg Kolpakov.

Free schedule.

The high cost of your info-products, at practically zero cost for their production.

Details about info *business:*

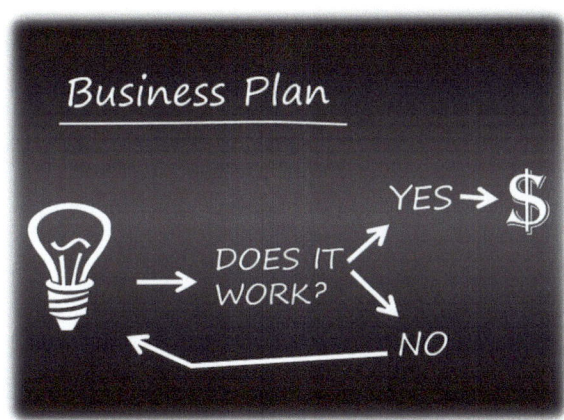

Info business is selling information products, training courses, eBooks, video courses, training.

Info business is divided into three categories:

 1. Distribution and resale of info-products of other developers.

2. Purchasing a license to resell and the affiliate program.

3.Creating and selling your own info-products.

We will do your authoring Info business the most profitable and most interesting!

If you're an expert or have knowledge in the field of traditional medicine, web design, cooking, etc.

Your information may be useful to other people. Be sure there are people who need this information and that it is looking for.

How do you convey this knowledge to people?

Can record your knowledge on DVV-ROM as course and offer it to people.

Rest assured, many will be interested in and will buy.

Now imagine this on a scale of millions of Internet users and you will understand how much you can earn!

The main plus of Business Info that you once create an info product and sell it for a very long time.

If your theme product info-sports, health, relationships, sex, it can be sold forever and get a good income!

Actually Info business, there's nothing particularly complex, opposite the very interesting.

Expert Email-Marketing
Oleg Kolpakov.

Info business can be done, as on an ongoing basis and give him 3-4 hours a day.

This is its popularity!

If you're new to Business Info and well-studied the recommendations on this topic, then after a few months, can reach the level of income of 300-500 dollars a month.

Because the whole world is your audience, there are no borders, this is the Internet!

It is important to engage in the business info you need at the beginning of "slow" day and night.

E-commerce success is diligence, hard work, patience and perseverance.

Expert Email-Marketing
Oleg Kolpakov.

Info business achieves success one who doesn't give up and continues to go to target.

Who wants to be successful, have to constantly seek and explore a variety of materials on business, advertising, email marketing, web design, etc.

Believe me, it's worth it. Is it bad to earn thousands of dollars a month sitting at home and love?

For example the average cost of your product info 20 dollars and multiplies those 20 dollars on a mass character of the Internet, and imagines possible earnings.

Now in the modern world, learning through video is one of the best and popular methods.

This method promotes the best assimilation of the material and at your fingertips. The teaching video course is present and the theory and practice.

People easier to buy one cheap training video course than ordering private tuition teachers.

They don't need any who adapts, may study at any convenient time, when there are a mood and desire.

Video course you can rewind and listen as much as you want or pause.

People don't need to go anywhere; you can study in a homelike atmosphere.

If you understand what you have to do, then go to the main study material!

Investments in business info:

Investment needs of the Internet business.

Without investment, the Internet cleverly engages in will not work.

Requires small attachments.

What expenses are required and that:

1) The cost of hosting and domain. Find a serious company and time-tested.

2) The cost of selling site and subscription page. Why selling the site, you need I think is understandable, but what is the subscription page, talk later.

Expert Email-Marketing
Oleg Kolpakov.

If you do not know how to create sites, you will have to either order the Freelancer or learn to do yourself.

Internets there are special services, where you can enjoy the beautiful and ready site or templates.

The most famous and proven service to me is **www.templatemonster.com**.

Here is a great selection of ready sites and templates. Create a quality website easily and not expensive.

3) You need to register with the service of reception and processing of orders when you create your own informational product. Need to automate this process.

Here the choice is yours, look for proven service.

4) Making costs of your product, product packaging, need Info business this 3D cover.

5) Major sales occur in the newsletters, you will need to connect to the special

service mailings that will store your subscription base.

By using the service you will perform all actions to this database.

The most popular and time-tested tools, service providers in developing and maintaining their own mailings, is

www.getresponse.com

This is an investment in your business that everyone can afford!

With theory and investment, we have finished, you can begin to practice:

OWN info PRODUCT:

Basically, beginner's info businessmen begin their path in the info business with anything, just not by creating your own info products.

Subscribe to various affiliate programs, sell other people's products and buy resale rights.

Try to go for a more easy way, don't want to create your own info products, hurry to earn and do not want to **spend time on their products, when already there whose ready.**

Most beginners think that in order to create info products need special skills, special knowledge, a special experience.

Afraid to start creating and failed to do so.

The first thing you should do: get rid of the thought "I can't." Just try and you will understand that it is accessible to absolutely everyone.

Expert Email-Marketing
Oleg Kolpakov.

Despite all the benefits of earning the partnership programs or the implementation of foreign products is still the basis of Info business is creating your own info products!

Be the author of your own product is nice and promising. Even if your first product will be cheaper than competitors and earn you less, but this is temporary.

That's when your own affiliate program will connect partners, and then your info product will gradually spread across the Internet.

The CHOICE of the THEME info product:

The first question that faces every beginner Info businessman is choosing a theme.

I will not give any tips; you better know what you know and what you like.

Ask yourself what course you want to create, ask yourself one more and the author of what course you want to be?

When you release your course, he will walk through the Internet, without your participation, aware of your name.

What topic to choose for your info product?

Go to any search engine to your browser and type in the search word: video and stroll through the directories of existing courses.

This is to ensure that you have expanded my horizon and saw a diverse world of training courses; you need to understand that there are no limitations.

Topics courses are completely different, from the masonry fireplaces

There are absolutely not popular topics, but these courses do exist, and their authors, they tested and checked rates on demand.

Think about how you want to take the whole day, take your time, make a list of all the topics on which you could create a training course.

The next step will be to verify these themes on demand.

You need to check whether your theme is interesting.

It may happen so that you have an interesting topic, but the demand for it on the Internet will be very low. Then there are

Accordingly, the sale will be very low. Need to find out.

Expert Email-Marketing
Oleg Kolpakov.

After you have tested and verified that the subject product is in demand, you can start creating your product info.

CREATE info PRODUCT:

To begin creating your info product, you need to decide on his model.

Info products are divided into three types:

1) A screencast video.

2) Live video.

3) EBooks.

Screencast video courses:

A screencast is a video lesson that was removed from your computer screen.

For example, you have a lesson on creating sites.

You consistently perform all the steps of creating a site, comment, and the program stores everything that was you on the screen, plus audio commentary.

You teach people the skills.

Live video:

The live video this video lesson, filmed on a video camera.

If you create a video course on fitness and you need live show how to correctly perform some exercise and of several such videos create VIDO-course.

E-books:

This option is the most famous on the Internet and the easiest.

Electronic books cheaper video courses.

They contain not less useful information and some even bigger and better bought because it is cheaper.

E-books are divided into three options: have been terminated abnormally- books, pdf books, and flash book.

1) EXE-eBooks-books created by the type of Web site and to view their browser are required.

2) PDF-books-these books are created in the program Microsoft Word or any other text editor and then saved in PDF format.

To view files in RDF format requires Adobe Reader.

3) FLASH-books-books with page turning effect, they are created in special programs, such as Flipping Book Publisher Viewer requires Flash Player.

Product model selection will primarily depend on the topic you have chosen. Because not every model is suitable for a particular subject.

When you choose the model of your product, you need to plan.

Which option to choose, you decide!

*Expert Email-Marketing
Oleg Kolpakov.*

We must remember that this is a paid product; this is a tutorial and must conform to all standards.

Website creation:

When you create your own info product, an important step would be to create a selling site!

Your website is your face and starts business info.

If the AU will not be a professional site, there will be no big sales.

If your website looks not professional, it will not be trusted and the visitor does not buy your product.

Mostly newbies make a free site for free templates, hurry to faster sell your course.

As a result sales. They throw Info business.

The main thing is to make a professional website!

How to get the most sales on your site?

Imagine you have a website and selling info product that we sell on this site.

You want to sell more and faster.

To do this, you apply all known ways to advertise to you, inviting you to our site, the maximum number of visitors and waiting for sales!

But very few sales.

You think that I have such a good product, you spent so much time on it and you're good all formalized, ordered advertising, what is it, why do so few sales?

Expert Email-Marketing
Oleg Kolpakov.

Such questions are asked by every newcomer in the info business.

Newcomers think, how do make your site visitors to buy.

That would answer this question; let's go through the whole chain of sales on your website, from start to finish.

Since entering, the visitor to the site and to order button.

Look at the whole process through the eyes of visitors, and ultimately find the main trump card, which will solve this problem.

There are five main points that affect the final decision of the visitor:

1) **IMPRESS a visitor:**

The first thing that draws the attention of the visitor by accessing the site is the site itself!

From the site depends on whether it will remain a visitor or immediately leaves him.

Sites must cling from the first second, and magically make the visitor view the information.

The site must be neat and stylish, evident.

The visitor will feel that the author of the site relates to their business seriously and won't run away from your site, and will scan it through.

Qualitatively new site, this is the first step to success!

2) Interest of the visitor:

Efforts, patience and hard work, you keep your visitor on your site. Now it's yours!

It means the interest visitors there are to your site!

Now a visitor will pay attention to the image of the product itself.

*Expert Email-Marketing
Oleg Kolpakov.*

Properly made cover your info product, has the attractive property causes the desire to see what's INSIDE, and this is a step towards a sale.

Cover, are more important than the site itself as if the site is a kind of platform for the product, the Visual image of this cover info product and subject to the opinion of the product.

Professionally made, attractive cover product info-this is another step to your success!

3) **Score of the visitor:**

For example, with the cover, you have everything in order.

She is brilliant and attractive and wants to see what is inside.

That's only after your visitor after seeing and appreciating your skin, intrigued by the contents, he returns to the top of the page, and are already beginning to explore in detail the advertising the text, with a view to learning in detail the contents of the product.

Expert Email-Marketing
Oleg Kolpakov.

Turns the page of the site down, slowly reads the text, gradually approaching the batting order.

Reads advertising text and the visitor realize that info product useful and interesting.

But suddenly he doubted! This often happens.

Here, you need a fourth time!

4) **Motivation and incentive:**

When a visitor questioned and could not take a decision, he needs a stimulus.

The best stimulus would be a bonus.

When a person understands that buying info product, it will give more useful visitors desired to buy increased and he buys.

Not always, other customers would do likewise and could not buy.

So what's the deal, how to solve this problem?

Expert Email-Marketing
Oleg Kolpakov.

Here you need the fifth element or discount!

5) **Promotion and Discount:**

Visitors of your site will cause the only limits!

Restrictions may be different.

For example, the restriction on the sale of the goods, together with a bonus. That is, along with the bonus item can only be purchased today.

The most important restriction is when the author declares that the goods can be bought only today or tomorrow the info of the product will be gone!

This method basically works, if the visitor, such items really need and postpone or think he no longer can.

Due to this, your sales will grow!

Expert Email-Marketing
Oleg Kolpakov.

This is the main method for success in business info!

Now we will explain how you all these proposals with restrictions to implement technically, competently and professionally!

When you spend releases, sales, promotions, discounts, you can set the countdown timer on the site.

Do ads start and end of the action and enjoy the result.
At the end of the promotion, or remove the timer and everything goes on as usual!

The rally was held, what next?

Create a newsletter with automatic series of letters and other automation tools.

You must configure the automation of its business process. Shares can be created every day.

To do so, when a visitor log in every day to your website could get you **LIMITED TIME OFFER**.

*Expert Email-Marketing
Oleg Kolpakov.*

That for him personally, starts a countdown timer indicating the end of the campaign.

And the main thing is that at the end of the promotion promised restrictions were implemented, i.e. access to them was closed.

This is important if promises are not honest and are not executed, they eventually stop responding.

To create the process, you need a good and proven script.

The script performs an important function. First, and most importantly, when you step into your site, the script sees and remembers the IP of the visitor.

Having fixed IP, it sends it to a special database which automatically creates.

The visitor remains in the database forever, unless you want to delete from there.

And most importantly, for each visitor, this process is different.

Expert Email-Marketing
Oleg Kolpakov.

On each site, at any time, day or night, in any region, this promotion and sale will encourage the visitor to purchase.

Now imagine how to increase your profits using you this tool.

On the Internet, locate and select the desired service, and install this script countdown timer showing the end of promotion for your website.

If you don't know how to install it, browse videos online, I will not dwell on this. Continue!

The administrative part:

1) PAYMENT SYSTEMS:

You have created your info product, formalized it, and prepared a selling site, now you can start the administrative parts of your business.

Your first step should be registered in payment systems.

A calculation on the Internet between you and the customers are electronic money.

Electronic money can pay for your goods to your customers.

Electronic money can pay for you, hosting, advertising, etc.

Electronic money is the equivalent of the usual plastic credit cards. This is the most convenient, reliable and promising tool of settlements via Internet.

The main convenience, it is easy to use and virtually instant exchange amounts between the parties.

If you decide to seriously engage in the Internet business, then you should definitely register major, the most common payment systems.

The most popular and trusted online payment systems:

1) **www.skrill.com**

2) **www.neteller.com**

3) **www.payza.com**

4) www.paypal.com

These payment systems are enjoyed all over the world.

After registering, you bind to your plastic card system, and the exchange of money takes place within these systems from card to card, between the parties.

The main thing is that the buyer and seller have been registered in this system.

These four payment systems are quite enough.

Here, each client will find a convenient way to pay.

Plug them into your site to pay for your courses visitors!

2) **Domain and Hosting:**

Once you have registered in payment systems, you will need to purchase a domain and hosting.

A domain is the name of the site on which people will find it on the Internet.

Choosing a domain name for your site, it is advisable to give the domain name that will fit in your activity and easily remembered.

Hosting is a service for hosting your Web site on a server hosting provider.

Hosting this is the place where your entire website files, in the 24-hour access.

Buy a domain and hosting only in proven areas!

In General, if you decide to do e-business seriously and for a long time, it is best to do from the outset, professional sites and share them for reliable hosting.

3) **VALID EMAIL:**

Email address is your signature and your logo will depend on the opinion of you as a professional.

It is important to register yourself a normal mailbox.

The simplest and most professional solution in this situation will connect the mailbox to your domain.

To do this, you can look on the Internet.

4)   **Sales:**

The sale of goods on the one-page sites, with the right approach and especially in conjunction with email marketing, can be much   more   efficient.

On a single-page website, the visitor does   not   scatter   eyes,from   the abundance of goods and there is no question "that choose", which leads more often to ensure that the visitor no buys.

The main thing that would be on the site turned out to be the target visitor, which are interested in this product, and he had only two choices to buys or not to buy.

A one-page site is best suited for business   info.

Business Info is the same; the buyer sees only a symbolic image of your product on the   site.

You cannot touch, taste, even just to see   "live",   and   the   visitor.

People need to be sure you really want what you're offering and useful product, and that it indeed contains the necessary information.

That the author knows something and is able to and that this is not just a beautiful picture   advertising.

Therefore,   you   should   give   some

material or a part of your free product sample.

You must first make a free product and give him so that people saw as your free materials.

It calls the credibility of the author, and then you can already offer people buy your main product.

This basic layout, which you should follow to achieve maximum results.

How to do on the Internet who offered free items?

For this purpose, there is email marketing. The fact of the matter is that your free product gives a reason, but in Exchange for his email.

The visitor first lands on your subscription page where you give him in Exchange for email offer something free to its interests.

Having received his email, you can build relationships and propose different both free and paid products.

This person becomes your subscriber, visitor voluntarily subscribes to your newsletter.

The Subscriber is not a casual visitor who visited your site.

A person who subscribes to your newsletter wants to receive information from you, it is interesting to your theme, and accordingly it is the potential of your customer!

To implement this technically, you need a subscription page, i.e. a one-page site.

The single-page site, there should be a description of your listings and subscription form.

Also, you need to connect to the service, which will store your entire subscription base, and with the help of which you will perform all actions to this database.

The most popular and time-tested Service providers in developing and maintaining their own mailings are service:

www.getresponse.com

Your newsletter is the most powerful means of exposure to potential customers.

Most importantly, what you need to start your sales is to create

subscription

page www.templatemonster.com, **create your own newsletter**

www.getresponse.com

and start to take the first steps to establish your own target audience-collect subscribers!

RECRUIT SUBSCRIPTION DATABASE:

Shag effective way sales in the Internet business, will be selling its own subscription base.

The main task of the Internet businessman is the constant increase and updates their subscription base.

Let's start with the most productive methods.

Where to start and what to do if you are a beginner?

Begin:

*Expert Email-Marketing
Oleg Kolpakov.*

1) **CONTEXTUAL ADVERTISING:**

Contextual advertising is a type of online advertising, which is based on the principle of consistency with the content of advertising material (content) The Web page that hosts this material.

Contextual advertising is important in marketing and is one of the most effective ways of advertising.

Be a powerful tool for promoting your website and sell your goods.

The most effective system of contextual advertising on the Web is Google AdWords.

Announcements broadcast on Google search or on the sites of affiliate network Google AdSense.

Contextual advertising is the most effective way of advertising because your potential customer has already made the first step, he has already made a request into a search engine on your topic, and you remain only to offer and sell its product. Contextual advertising gives you high-quality subscribers.

The Subscriber must be purposeful and not subscribe because he liked your subscription page and because of he really interested in your topic.

This point must always be you're main in finding subscribers!

Contextual advertising gives you targeted subscribers.

Subscribers go to you. They've already taken the first step by typing a query into the search bar, you only need to correctly configure the ad campaign.

Contextual advertising is the most expensive and complicated system.

Have its own unique strategy and strong competition.

You have two options to start the contextual advertising.

1) Use the services of professionals who, for a fee, will keep all your campaigns. But it is worth it is expensive.

2) To buy courses and learn the whole system itself, but also contextual advertising courses are not cheap.

3) Find free information on the Internet and start yourself, try to run contextual advertising. Learn from their mistakes.

This is a great topic and should be studied separately; I will not dwell on this.

2) **Advertising in newsletter:**

Advertising in newsletter, quick and efficient way to recruit subscribers and also paid, but much cheaper than PPC advertising.

How does it work?

Your main goal, in this case, looks for a mailing with your theme and only targeted subscribers.

When the order ad in the newsletter, you must agree with the advertiser to the letter should only be your advertisement, no third-party banner ads, and links, otherwise, the return on such advertising will be significantly less!

Another important point on which most beginners make mistakes, order mailing list with a large number of subscribers.

Newbies on the inexperience of looking for big mailing to sell more and earn big money.

Unfortunately, in most cases such mailings "dead".

The fact of the matter is that such mailings old and most subscribers have long lost interest in the author and the subject.

In e-mails, which is often given someone else's advertising, opening letters are bad, better about mailing more 5000 people, forget at all.

You have to look for a mailing list with a small amount of 1000-1500 maximum subscribers, this newsletter is always fresh and the people here are not tortured, the main thing is not too expensive.

Search the Internet, proven and high-quality services for your mailing **advertising in the newsletter**.

3) INTER-PUBLIC RELATIONS:

Inter-PR, this is when two similar subjects, at the same time give each other's ads in their newsletters.

This method has pros and cons.

A plus is that it's free.

Minus the fact that giving someone else's advertisement in its database, you divide your subscribers with another author, and if

It is best to carry out **inter-PR** 1-2 times a month, carefully choose partners, do not advertise on their basis of bad publicity!

When you negotiate **inter-PR**, be sure to ask the last two screenshots of emails it to watch the opening mailing letters to show that his base live.

4) **Viral marketing:**

This method, I like best because here you don't need to do anything.

Its meaning is that you reward which the training course, for example, ask for an invite in its distribution database, a certain number of subscribers.

The technical organization of this process is carried out in special services.

You charge into an automated series of letters to his proposal, connected to the service, and it revolves itself around, collecting subscriber database.

Find online services such VIRAL MARKETING!

5) AFFILIATE PROGRAM:

This method can be used only by those who already have something to sell.

Affiliate marketing is effective only if you have good partners, knowing their business.

These partners can give you more traffic than all of the above methods.

But to get such partners.

The Board you are not yet, hurries up

with the affiliate program.

Creating your first info product, you do not need to directly connect to it an **affiliate program**, no matter how remarkable it seemed.

First, sell it; make sure your info product is in demand.

To get started with your partners, you need to prepare advertising and auxiliary material: banners, emails, ads, affiliate links.

Create a course, instruction for your future partners, to work in your **affiliate program**.

Once you have a new partner, contact them, and socialize.

Learn beginner or experienced its partner, ask him, need him training or promotional material.

This attitude with your partners gives a serious   result.

Affiliate marketing can be a powerful tool, both in sales and in the set of subscribers.

6)   **SOCIAL   NETWORKS:**

Social networking is a huge source of traffic. Almost every Internet user, there is an account in which neither whether the social   network.

But get it out of there, not just traffic!

People in social networks come to buy or learn, and they are absolutely not interested in advertising on this human interest in social networks the hardest.

How to extract traffic from social networks?

1) **Targeting advertising** is an advertising mechanism, which allows the user to select from all available audience only the part that you need.

Targeting, contextual advertising, and analog here as in context have their own strategies and secrets.

Targeting, as well as Direct, you need to learn.

2) **Advertising in groups and communities.**

Each group has its own theme, respectively, and the audience it is going to.

If the group is not yet popular and not scored a large number of subscribers, advertising can be given for free.

If a group has a large number of subscribers, group's administrators will take over the advertising money.

3) **Social exchanges are mediators between administrators groups and advertisers.**

Through **social exchanges** to advertise easier, because all they have contacts already established, costs are known, you need only select the desired group in the directory.

Find on the Internet, such social exchange.

4) **Bulletin boards-the easiest way you can absolutely free to give any ads**. You and paid it is efficient.

7) **Comments**:

Comment this is another powerful source of traffic.

How does it work?

1) **From the comments,** this is the widget that social network.

The comment that takes the visitor to the website or blog, this form will be posted on the wall appears his account on a social network, it sees all his friends.

If his friends will be interested in the post, then they move on to link the site, where he posted a **comment**.

This method gives a good advertisement of your site.

If you're still and encourage your site visitors to leave **comments** to any article, then there will be more **comments** and traffic respectively.

But do it in the next letter after you subscribe.

2) **You yourself are leaving comments on what the foreign sites**.

The point is that in the **comment**, you

are sure to add a link to my site or subscription page.

The effect can be quite impressive, as some blogs have hundreds and even thousands of visitors per day. But here you need to follow a few rules.

You have to understand that site owners do not love, if their site is used as an advertising platform, and your comment may be deleted.

How to avoid it?

Need to write a **comment** so that the owner of a site or blog, I didn't want to delete it.

Write a positive review about the article or about the site.
The comment must be literate, and consist of several proposals.

Write a **comment**, so that customers are interested in you and want to know more about you.

Or a simpler option is at the end of the **comment**, direct appeal to familiarize themselves with the same article or resource on your link.

This method is ideal for beginner info business to gain its first subscribers, most importantly this method is complimentary!

8) **BANNER ADVERTISING**:

Banner advertising on every page on the Internet.

The result from such advertising is not large, but with the right approach, the result is good.

To banner advertising to be effective, you need a website or resource with good attendance.

Still, depends on your banner, you need a good and beautiful views.

A resource that will host the banner, you need to understand that the higher attendance, the higher the price of accommodation.

When choosing a site for advertising, you need to keep in mind four points: attendance of the resource, the approximate conversions on banner exchange and the value of your product.

On the Internet, you can find many **Exchange banner advertising.**

When you create a banner, not only affects the appearance of the transitions, but also information that is written on it, it should be of interest to visitors.

The appearance of the banner should be taken seriously, if you do not own a graphics editor, then it is better to buy a banner. **www.graphicriver.net , cheap and a great choice!**

9) **TEASER advertising**:

The teaser is provocative, teasing and games advertising that attracts the attention of consumers.

To place a teaser, you need to use the services of a company teaser.

TEASER company cooperates with webmasters and have a network of advertising platforms.

The Internet can easily find TEASER company.

Teaser you can order here, teasernet.com.

Expert Email-Marketing
Oleg Kolpakov.

10) **Technical means**:

   Technical tools to attract subscribers.

   1) " **ComeBacker**" is a programming code that is installed on your site and it works as follows.

When a visitor wants to close the page by clicking on the "close" button at the top of the screen, the window opens with a call to stay and receive a gift.

 Such a call, you can write what you want. There is also a voice option, together with the text of your appeal will be voiced by voice.

  In the back, at the same time, shows another page, on which you recommend to stay.

   " **ComeBacker**" is set on selling the site, and after closing the man gets on the subscription page. Not bought, so,signed up.

   Recommend you to buy this "**ComeBacker**" for your site.

2) "**Pop-up**" window does not appear after you close the page, and when a visitor is going to close the page and crosses the upper line of the browser.

Page remains the same, simply darken the background around the window.

Free "Pop-up" window can be found on the Internet.

3) **Social Castle "was not designed to retain customers, namely to attract new ones.**

How does it work?

«Social» Castle, this code, which is set in the page where you offer a gift.

But the link to get this gift is closed thereby **locking**, and so she became available, the visitor must click on one of the buttons of social networks.

After he clicks, the lock opens, the link becomes available, and on the wall of a social network, you receive a link to your site.

Expert Email-Marketing
Oleg Kolpakov.

As a result, the visitor receives your gift, and your new visitors and everyone is happy.

An online search for **"Social" Castle** and be sure to install on your site!

11) **Video is hosting**:

Between articles and video on the same subject, a person chooses the video.

Some information cannot be present in the text version.

Posting video on **video is hosted**, is another source of traffic.

This method requires some work. Just place the video, add a description with a link to your resource, is not enough.

The video you want to promote, raise by rating, constantly work to increase views. In General is a great theme, need to learn from a book or course.

Find online **popular video is hosting** websites and start to quietly explore them.

12) **OWN BLOG**:

Own blog if they seriously engaged, will bring you much more subscribers than all of the above methods.

Visitors who will visit your blog says that you and your information of interest to them.

Mon blog brings them benefits.

This will be no subscribers, your friends, and they are more likely to buy than others.

To get a result from their own blog, they need to be addressed, it should appear regular updates so that people were hunting   for   him   to   return.

To create a good blog, it takes a long time.

A blog needs to advance in the search engine.

It's called **SEO-optimized**, and need to understand   or   hire   a   professional.

SEO-search engine optimization is a complex of measures for raising of site positions in search engines results for some users, with the aim of promoting the site.

Just so no one will see your blog, you need   to   spin.

Blog if you want to register in the catalogs, you will need to be active, to be engaged   in   advertising   promotion.

The first step is registration of blog promotion blog to search engines and subject   directories.

Blog registration is necessary for it to find as many people as possible to your potential customers.

Through the search engines, your blog users find direct topical searches.

Through catalogs, thanks to categorization, your blog resides strictly in a specific order directory, related to the topic of interest to the visitor.

Registration can be carried out in manual mode or by means of special programs.

The most affordable and convenient way will register with the help of the special services desk.

On the Internet, there are many such services, can find if you decide to create your blog.

In such services, you can manually register yourself and for free, or give this case service professional, saving your own time, but it's scramble a.

The next step of promotion of your blog will be registering in the rankings and increase   visits.

 Registration in the ratings by importance comes in second place, after registration in search engines and directories.

 The more your blog is visited, the higher you are in the ranking, which means growing attendance and your rating.

Create a blog, the process is complex. If you don't have time, it's better not to start. This blog is a great theme.

13)   **TIPS   for   beginners**:

We looked at all of the most effective, ways to set subscription base.

Now, let's look at another point: where to start and how to precede, if he have no experience at all, and most importantly, money.

The very first thing that I wish I could advise you before you recruit subscribers to get a newsletter service www.getresponse.com.

If you create a newsletter, you can begin to recruit subscribers!

If you start with the absolute zero, then the easiest and quickest way to recruit subscribers will be advertising in a mailing list, but the money you don't have, or you just don't want them to invest.

In this case, you need to act differently.

First of all, I would recommend comments, this is the most time-consuming way, but it is totally free and works well.

You need to find on the Internet, as many blogs and resources on your topic and post their comments if there is such a possibility.

Expert Email-Marketing
Oleg Kolpakov.

Write literate comment links to the subscription page, do not be lazy and the result will be forthcoming!

The next option is the ads in social networks.

First of all, you need to filter the community and group on your topic and post your ads in them.

Need it each day, as many advertisers, and advertising in a few hours will be far below, where no one will see it.

Do not forget about the message boards.

Such methods allow you to, for short term gain at least 300-400 subscribers!

Viral marketing will give your subscribers itself, you do not need to do anything.

The only problem might be the availability of the product for distribution.

Here there are two options: Create something you or by someone else's info product with resale rights.

Online for sale a lot of courses with resale rights, you can easily buy any not expensive info product.

Using all of these methods, you must dial a couple of months its first 1000 Subscribers.

With thousands of subscribers you have and PR will be serious, and it is already possible to sell.

You can sell products on an affiliate program and earn the first money on advertising in the newsletter.

Now you can proceed to the most efficient method for advertising in the newsletter.

Advertising in newsletters should immediately pay off. Therefore, by this time, you should already be valuable info product that you'll offer immediate after the activation of the subscription.

Info product must be valuable, because it is the first sale and depended on the man, will the customer buy from you in the future.

Best of all, the first info product to sell during the subscription, inexpensive.

Cheap info products will sell well and your advertising will pay off, and yet earn.

Subscriber bought at such a low price product that value worth many times more expensive in the future can buy you something else already more expensive info product or goods.

An important point you need your first marketing proposal do exactly when you activate the subscription, rather than the first letter after.

The address of the site from the selling proposition must be specified in the paragraph: "the website address after activation" mailing service.

Acting in such methods, you'll move forward faster steps, most importantly to respect stability and permanence.

Testing each method individually, you'll Act, relying on their own experience, that over time you will have.

Use all these methods at the same time, and give them due attention, you certainly won't be able to, it's just physically impossible.

Therefore, you should regularly test each method and put first the most effective options.

Expert Email-Marketing
Oleg Kolpakov.

Continuous testing and integration of statistics, this your key to success!

For statistics, there is a special

service: www.google.com/analytics.

On the Internet, you can find and watch videos, detailing will show how and where track the effectiveness of channel subscriber's service

www.google.com/analytics.

QUICK LAUNCH:

What is info business? We found with the theory and practice of figured out too.

There's another branch in info business, which avoids many difficulties and starts much faster!

How make you run faster?

*Expert Email-Marketing
Oleg Kolpakov.*

All the basic info, business organization can be divided into two parts:

1) **Creating a product for sale, product decoration, Website creation for sale**.

2) **Configuring administration, business process, connects the required services**.

The easiest solution will be to buy a ready-made product; this method is called **business info-RESSELING**.

Creating your own info product and think whether he claimed as you like, or whether it ever sold.

These thoughts plagued all beginners. Better yet would be to buy the finished product, configure all administration and selling it.

In the meantime, feel free to create your own product.

From quick-start business info a lot of pluses, but the most important is that

Expert Email-Marketing
Oleg Kolpakov.

selling someone else's product you receives experience.

Because not everything in the first stage, you will have received, and all the initial bugs better do on foreign products.

When you finally will create an info product and you will already have experience in advertising and sales online, you will be able to declare to the whole world about his own brand.

Resseling this is a quick and smart start.

To buy a product with resale rights, you need to enter in the search bar of your browser, the phrase "**resseling products**", and will give you a list of sites with such proposals.

It depends on you whether you want to start small, or purchase the expensive and popular product.

The most important thing when buying a product, do no forget about testing it on demand, how doing, we already were!

Expert Email-Marketing
Oleg Kolpakov.

Conclusion:

The dear reader *concludes our great training.*

 Thank you *for your choice and confidence in this book.*

 I hope that the material that you read will help you run your business on the Internet.

Apply all methods in practice and you achieve success in your business info!

 I wish you a quick and successful launch, profitable business, and human happiness.

 Can leave your feedback about the book, it is important for me to know that my work has not gone in vain.

 I thank you in advance.

With a deep respect: Oleg Kolpakov.

www.ingramcontent.com/pod-product-compliance
Lightning Source LLC
Chambersburg PA
CBHW040833180526
45159CB00001B/170